P9-DNG-301

Slave Narratives
THE JOURNEY TO FREEDOM
Elaine Landau

In Their Own Voices

FRANKLIN WATTS • A DIVISION OF GROLIER PUBLISHING
NEW YORK • HONG KONG • SYDNEY • DANBURY, CONNECTICUT

FOR ALEXANDER GARMIZO

Cover: a slave woman picking cotton
Title page: *On to Liberty* by Theodor Kaufmann

Photographs ©: Archive Photos: 18, 19, 24 inset, 30 right, 36, 40, 44, 56, 57, 68 right, 87;
Bridgeman Art Library International Ltd., London/New York: 1 (CH 92951/ Private Collection/
Christie's Images), 60 (MGS 120609/ Private Collection), (MGS 120603, Private Collection);
Brown Brothers: 14 inset, 31 bottom, 39; Corbis-Bettmann: 49; Culver Pictures: 22 (C. Seaver
Jr.), cover, 14, 30 left, 61, 68 left; Duke University, Durham, NC: 4 bottom, 71, 73 (Rare Book,
Manuscript, & Special Collections Library); North Wind Picture Archives: 16, 22 inset, 24, 27,
31 middle, 31 top, 45, 51, 65, 67, 82, 83; Stock Montage, Inc.: 6, 9; University of North Car-
olina at Chapel Hill, Academic Affairs Library: 3 bottom, 35 (from "Thirty Years a Slave" by
Louis Hughes), 3 top, 13 (from "Twenty-Two Years a Slave, and Forty Years a Freeman" by Austin
Steward), 4 top, 55 (from "The Narrative of Bethany Veney: A Slave Woman").

Illustration and chapter openers by: Vilma Ortiz Dillon

Library of Congress Cataloging-in-Publication Data

Slave narratives: the journey to freedom / [compiled] by Elaine Landau.
        p.cm. – (In their own voices)
    Austin Steward – Louis Hughes – Bethany Veney – James L. Smith.
Includes bibliographical references (p.) and index.
ISBN 0-531-11743-X
    1. Slaves—United States—Biography—Juvenile literature. 2. Fugitive slaves—United
States—Biography—Juvenile literature. 3. Afro-Americans—Biography—Juvenile literature.
4. Slaves' writings, American—Juvenile literature. [1. Slaves. 2. Afro-Americans—Biography.
3. Slavery.] 1. Landau, Elaine. II. In their own voices (Franklin Watts, Inc.)

E444. S565 2001
973'.0496073'00922—dc21
[B]   00-32515

CONTENTS

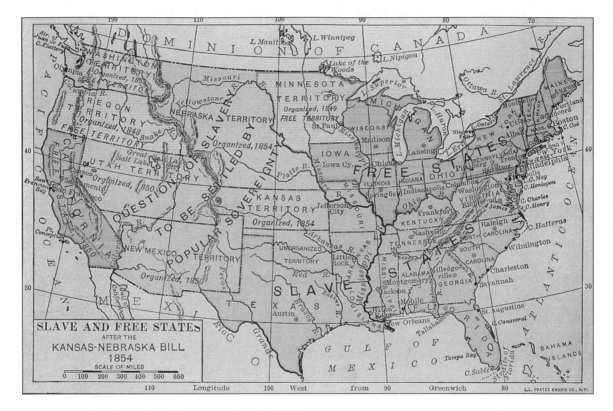

The states where Slavery was legal in 1854

INTRODUCTION

"Saturday night came. I knew well that, if not caught . . . Jerry would be round. At last everyone was in bed, and all was still. I waited and listened. . . . Then I heard his step at the door. I hurriedly opened it, and he came in. His clothes were still damp and stiff from the rain yesterday. He was frightened and uneasy. He had been hiding around in different places, fearing detection. . . ."

These are the words of a former slave. Her husband, Jerry, who was also a slave but who was owned by a different master, had run away. He had just learned that his owner was about to sell him. In the end, the couple determined that there was no way out; he would be sold. Pregnant at the time, the woman knew that once he was sold, she would never see her husband again.

In today's world, it is difficult to imagine what being a slave in America must have been like. However, during Slavery, slaves were told from birth that they were valued only as a piece of property. At any moment a member of their family could be sold off. They worked from dawn to dusk while they lived in a shack with barely enough food and clothing. They were subjected to beatings, rape, or torture at another person's whim.

Slavery was a well-established, if brutal, aspect of the South's economy. Putting its inhumanity aside, there were obvious economic advantages to slave ownership. The slave remained in bondage for life as well as the slave's children, adding to the slaveholder's long term investment.

The challenge to slave owners was to have slaves do their bidding. To effectively accomplish that, slaves had to fear brutal punishments or even death as a consequence of defiance. The owners had little to fear under this system. If a slave died while being punished, usually the only penalty was the loss of property.

It is remarkable that any slave enduring these terrible conditions had the inner strength to fight back—yet many did. Slaves rose up against their masters in armed rebellions. Among the best known of these was Nat Turner's slave rebellion in Virginia in the summer of 1831. Led by Turner, fewer than one hundred slaves conducted a two-day insurrection in which fifty-five whites were killed. The rebels were hanged, but they had been willing to take their chances rather than remain slaves.

Slaves rebelled in quiet ways, too, and some even made their way to freedom. We can read about what life was like for such individuals and other African-Americans before the Civil War through firsthand accounts of former slaves. Known as slave narratives, these autobiographies span a broad range of experiences. Some accounts document the backbreaking labor on cotton plan-

The discovery of Nat Turner after the rebellion

tations in the Deep South. Others tell of working in the homes of slave owners. All attest to the horrors of this unjust system.

This book contains excerpts from four slave narratives. Parts of these stories may be difficult to read. Their content is unsettling, while the writing style of the era is stiffer and more artificial than the way we speak and write today. Therefore, while reading them, it is important not to lose sight of the story behind the words.

Admittedly, the slaves who wrote these narratives were not typical. Possessing incredible fortitude and the right amount of luck, they eventually gained their freedom. Their stories may be known as slave narratives, but they are actually much more. They are tales of bravery, resourcefulness, and determination in the face of overwhelming odds.

Austin Steward

PART ONE

At the Great House

Born into slavery in 1794, Austin Steward's life was unusual from the start. As a youth he had been chosen to work at the plantation owner's home and had luckily escaped the backbreaking field labor of the plantation. Slaves who worked in their master's homes often had easier lives. But such situations varied from place to place. Although house slaves did not work long hours under the hot sun, they were still frequently beaten by their owners for every minor, or even imagined, wrongdoing.

I was born in Prince William County, Virginia. At seven years of age, I found myself a slave on the plantation of Capt. William Helm. Our family consisted of my father and mother—whose names were Robert and Susan Steward—a sister, Mary, and myself. As the usual custom, we lived in a small cabin built of rough boards, with a floor of earth, and small openings in the sides of the cabin were substituted for windows. The chimney was built of sticks and mud; the door, of rough boards; and the whole was put together in the rudest possible manner. As to the furniture of this rude dwelling, it was procured by the slaves themselves. I never knew Capt. H. to furnish his slaves with household utensils of any description.

Austin Steward

The amount of provision given out on the plantation per week was invariably one peck of corn or meal for each slave. This allowance was given in meal when it could be obtained; when it could not, they received corn, which they pounded in mortars after they returned from their labor in the field. The slaves on our plantation were provided with very little meat. In addition to the pack of corn or meal, they were allowed a little salt and a few herrings. If they wished for more, they were obliged to earn it by overwork. They were permitted to cultivate small gardens, and were thereby enabled to provide themselves with many trifling conveniences. But these gardens were only allowed to some of the more industrious. Capt. Helm allowed his slaves a small quantity of meat during harvest time, but when the harvest was over they were obliged to fall back on the old allowance.

When eight years of age, I was taken to the "great house," or the family mansion of my master, to serve as an errand boy, where I had to stand in the presence of my master's family all

Slaves lived in small cabins built with wooden boards and logs. There were few comforts.

the day, and part of the night, ready to do anything which they commanded me to perform. . . .

Capt. Helm was not a very hard master; but generally was kind and pleasant. Indulgent when in good humor, but like many of the Southerners, terrible when in a passion. He was a great sportsman, and very fond of company. He generally kept one or two race horses, and [a] pack of hounds for fox-hunting. He was not only a sportsman, but a gamester, and was in the *habit of playing cards, and sometimes betting very high and losing accordingly.*

Mrs. Helm was a very industrious woman, and generally busy in her household affairs—sewing, knitting, and looking after the servants; but she was a great scold, continually finding fault with some of the servants, and frequently punishing the young slaves herself, by striking them over the head with a heavy iron key, until the blood ran; or else whipping them with a cowhide [whip], which she always kept by her side when sitting in her room. The older servants she would cause to be punished by having them severely whipped by a man, which she never failed to do for every trifling fault. I have felt the weight of some of her heaviest keys on my own head, and for the slightest offenses.

No slave could possibly escape being punished—I care not how attentive they might be, nor how industrious. . . . Mrs. Helm appeared to be uneasy unless some of the servants were under the lash.

In one such instance, Steward was forced to watch his owner's irrational rage taken out on his mother. That day his mother, who cooked for the family, had begun making dinner when Mrs. Helm came in to check on things. While there, Mrs. Helm rubbed one of the ceramic pots so hard with a cloth that it cracked. The sight of the damaged pot so infuriated her that she called for her husband. Instead of blaming herself, she had her husband whip Steward's mother. Steward briefly described this account:

Young slaves who served inside the master's home always stood close by their master. They quickly fetched anything the master needed, such as food or drink.

That [cracked pot] was enough to invoke the wrath of my master, who came forth immediately with his horse-whip, with which he whipped my poor mother most unmercifully—far more severely than I ever knew him to whip a horse . . . And yet Capt. Helm was not the worst of masters. . . .

When I was not employed as an errand-boy, it was my duty to stand behind my master's chair, which was sometimes the whole day, never being allowed to sit in his presence. Indeed, no slave is ever allowed to sit down in the presence of their master or mistress. If a slave is addressed when sitting, he is required to spring to his feet, and instantly remove his hat, if he has one, and answer in the most humble manner, or lay the foundation for a flogging, which will not be long delayed.

I slept in the same room with my master and mistress. This room was elegantly furnished with damask curtains, mahogany bedstead of the most expensive kind, and every thing else about it was of the most costly kind. And while [Capt.] and Mrs. Helm reposed on their bed of down, with a cloud of lace floating over them, like some Eastern Prince, with their slaves to fan them while they slept, and to tremble when they awoke, I always slept upon the floor, without a pillow or even a blanket, but, like a dog, lay down anywhere I could find a place.

CHAPTER TWO

Moving North

Due to poor business choices and excessive gambling, Captain Helm was forced to sell his plantation and some of his slaves. Austin Steward was among the remaining ones he took with him to New York State.

After the sale of the plantation, Capt. Helm was in possession of quite a large sum of money, and having never paid much attention to his pecuniary interests [money], he acted as if there could be no end of it. He realized about forty thousand dollars from the sale of his estate in Virginia, which would have been a pretty sum in the hands of a man who had been accustomed to look after his own interests; but under the management of one who had all his life lived and prospered on the unrequited [unpaid] toil of slaves, it was of little account. He bought largely of every thing he thought necessary for himself or the comfort of his family, for which he always paid the most extravagant prices. The Captain was not as well qualified to take care of himself and family as some of his slaves were; but he thought different, and so the preparations for leaving the old plantation for a home in the wilds of New York went on under his discretion. . . .

Capt. Helm had determined to leave his family until he could get his slaves settled in their future quarters, and a home provided for himself, when they were expected to join him. We traveled northward, through Maryland, Pennsylvania, and a portion of New York, to Sodus Bay, where [we] halted for some time. We made about twenty miles per day, camping out every night, and reached that place after a march of twenty days. Every morning the overseer called the roll, when every slave must answer to his or her name, felling to the ground with his cowhide any delinquent who failed to speak out in quick time.

The slaves' quarters, a small group of cabins, was the area on the plantation where the slaves lived.

After the roll had been called, and our scanty breakfast eaten, we marched on again, our company presenting the appearance of some numerous caravan crossing the desert of Sahara. When we pitched our tents for the night, the slaves must immediately set about cooking not their supper only, but their breakfast, so as to be ready to start early the next morning, when the tents were struck; and we proceeded on our journey in this way to the end.

Capt. Helm still continued to take the oversight of his slaves, and was out every day, superintending his business, just as his overseer used to do. About this time a man named Henry Tower came to hire "slave boys," as we were called. The Captain hired to him Simon and myself. . . .

Mr. Tower had just bought a tract of land, [and] contemplated making great improvements, building mills, opening stores, etc. This tract of land was comparatively wild, there being but a small frame house for a dwelling, one for a store, and another for a blacksmith shop. The firm [Mr. Tower's] had a great number of men in their employ that year. I was kept busy helping the women about the cooking

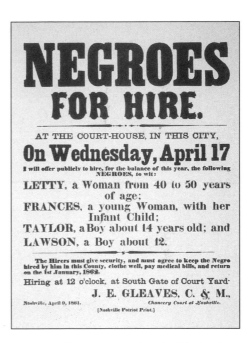

Some slave owners advertised in local newspapers to hire out their slaves.

and housework. And here, for the first time in my life, I had a comfortable bed to sleep on, and plenty of wholesome food to eat; which was something both new and strange to me.

I continued to live with the Towers; and in the fall of that year, I had the misfortune to cut my foot badly. Dr. Taylor was immediately called, [but] . . . I have been slightly lame from that day to this. For several weeks I was unable to be moved, and was regularly attended by Dr. Taylor, but as soon as it could be done without danger, I was taken back to Capt. Helm's, where I found things in much the same condition as when I left them over a year before. . . .

But the kind treatment I had always received from the Messrs. Tower and family made it very hard for me to reconcile myself to my former mode of living; especially now that I was lame and weak, from sickness and long confinement; besides, it was cold weather. Oh! how hard it did seem to me, after having a good bed and plenty of bed clothes every night for so long a time, to now throw myself down, like a dog, on the "softest side" of a rough board, without a pillow, and without a particle of bedding to cover me during the long cold nights of winter. To be reduced from a plentiful supply of good, wholesome food, to the mere pittance which the Captain allowed his slaves, seemed to me beyond endurance.

New Beginnings

CHAPTER THREE

. . . I had always lived and fared thus, but I never felt so bitterly these hardships and the cruelties of Slavery as I did at that time; making a virtue of necessity, however, I turned my thoughts in another direction.

I managed to purchase a spelling book, and set about teaching myself to read, as best I could. Every spare moment I could find was devoted to that employment, and when about my work I could catch now and then a stolen glance at my book, just to refresh my memory with the simple lesson I was trying to learn. . . .

It finally reached the ears of my master that I was learning to read; and then, if he saw me with a book or a paper in my hand, oh, how he would swear at me, sending me off in a hurry, about some employment. Still I persevered, but was more careful about being seen making any attempt to learn to read. At last, however, I was discovered, and had to pay the penalty of my determination.

One of the penalties that the slaves endured was a whipping or flogging. Sometimes this left permanent scars on a slave's body.

I had been set to work in the sugar bush, and I took my spelling book with me. When a spare moment occurred, I sat down to study and so absorbed was I in the attempt to blunder through my lesson, that I did not hear the Captain's son-in-law coming until he was fairly upon me. He sprang forward, caught my poor old spelling book, and threw it into the fire, where it was burned to ashes; and then came my turn. He gave me first a severe flogging, and then swore if he ever caught me with another book, he would "whip every inch of skin off my back." . . . This treatment, however, instead of giving me the least idea of giving it up, only made me look upon it as a more valuable attainment.

. . . About this time Capt. Helm began to sell off his slaves to different persons, as he could find opportunity, and sometimes at a great sacrifice. It became apparent that the Captain, instead of prospering in business, was getting poorer every day.

After living sometime in Bath . . . I began to think that it was possible for me to become a free man in some way . . . as I had often thought of doing. I had listened to the conversation of others, and determined to ask legal counsel on the subject the first opportunity I could find.

Very soon after, as I was drawing wood, I met on the river bridge, Mr. D. Cruger, the eminent lawyer . . . and I asked him to tell me if I was not free, by the laws of New York. . . . [The laws governing the status of slaves varied in different parts of the country.]

I sought another opportunity to speak with Mr. Cruger, and at last found him in his office alone; then he conversed freely on the subject of Slavery, telling me that Capt. Helm could not hold me as a slave in that State, if I chose to leave him, and then directed me to D. Comstock and J. Moore; the first being at the head of a Manumission society [a humanitarian group that assisted those illegally kept as slaves] and the last named gentleman one of its directors.

Although in many ways Steward's life was superior in the North to what it had been on the plantation, he along with others of Captain Helm's slaves were determined to be free.

THE LIBERATOR.

WILLIAM LLOYD GARRISON AND ISAAC KNAPP, PUBLISHERS. [NO. 22.

OUR COUNTRY IS THE WORLD—OUR COUNTRYMEN ARE MANKIND. [SATURDAY, MAY 28, 1831.

William Lloyd Garrison was a printer, journalist, and abolitionist in Boston. He published many articles in his newspaper *The Liberator* about freeing slaves and ending Slavery.

Everywhere that Slavery exists, it is nothing but slavery. I found it just as hard to be beaten over the head with a piece of iron in New York as it was in Virginia.

I had determined to make an effort to own myself, and as a preliminary step, I obtained permission of Capt. Helm to visit some friends living in Canandaigua and Geneva [northern New York State]. This was in the winter of 1814. . . . I called on James Moore, as directed by Mr. Cruger, and found he was one of the directors of the "Manumission Society," as it was then called. This was an association of humane and intelligent gentlemen whose object it was to aid any one who was illegally held in bondage. The funds of the society were ample; and able counsel was employed to assist those who needed it. . . . I soon got an interview with Mr. Moore, to whom I related the history of my life—the story of my wrongs and hardships. I told him about my having been hired out by Capt. Helm, which he said was sufficient to insure my freedom.

As Moore interpreted New York State law, when Captain Helm hired Steward out in that state, Captain Helm lost his right of ownership.

He [Moore] said that indispensable business called him to Albany, where he must go immediately, but assured me that he would return in March following; then I must come to him and he would see that I had what justly belonged to me—my freedom from Slavery. He advised me to return to Bath and go on with my work as usual until March, but to say nothing of my intentions and prospects. . . .

I went cheerfully back to my labor, and worked with alacrity, impatient only for March to come; and as the time drew near I began to consider what kind of an excuse I could make to get away. I could think of none, but I determined to go without one, rather than to remain.

So Close to Freedom

CHAPTER FOUR

Just before the time appointed for me to meet Mr. Moore, a slave girl named Milly, came secretly to Bath. She had been one of Capt. Helm's slaves, and he had a while before sold her to a man who lived some distance west of the village. Milly had now taken the matter into her own hands. She had left her master to take care of himself, and was in short "running away," determined as myself, that she would be a slave no longer; resolved on death, or freedom from the power of the slaveholder.

The time I had set for my departure was so near at hand, that I concluded to accompany her in her flight. When the dark night came on, we started together, and traveled all night, and just as the day dawned we arrived at Manchester, where we stopped a short time with one Thomas Watkins.

But, I was not to be let go so easily. I had been missed at Capt. Helm's and several men started in immediate pursuit. I was weary, and so intent on getting a little rest that I did not see my pursuers until they had well nigh reached the house where I was; but I did see them in time to spring from the house with the agility of a deer, and to run for the woods as for life. And indeed, I so considered it. I was unarmed to be sure, and not prepared to defend myself against two or three men, armed to the teeth; but it would have gone hard with me before I surrendered myself to them, after having dreamed as I had, and anticipated the blessings of a free man. I escaped them, thank God, and reached the woods, where I concealed myself for some time. . . .

As soon as I thought it prudent, I pursued my journey, and finally came out into the open country, near the dwelling of Mr. Dennis Comstock, who, as I have said, was president of the

Slaves usually ran away from their owners during the night. This drawing shows a large group of slaves escaping together.

Manumission Society. To him I freely described my situation, and found him a friend indeed. He expressed his readiness to assist me, and wrote a line for me to take to his brother, Otis Comstock, who took me into his family at once. I hired to Mr. Comstock for the season, and from that time onward lived with him nearly four years.

When I arrived there I was about twenty-two years of age, and felt for the first time in my life, that I was my own master. I cannot describe to a free man, what a proud manly feeling came over me when I hired to Mr. C. and made my first bargain, nor when I assumed the dignity of collecting my own earnings. . . . I was very happy in my freedom from Slavery, and had a good home, where for the first time in my life I was allowed to sit at table with others. . . .

When I had been with Mr. Comstock about a year, we received a visit from my old master, Capt. Helm, who had spared no pains to find me, and when he learned where I was he came to claim me as "his boy," who he said he "wanted and must have."

Mr. Comstock told him I was not "his boy," and as such he would not give me up; and further, that I was free by the laws of the state. He assured the Captain that his hiring me out in the first instance, to Mr. Tower, forfeited his claim to me, and gave me a right to freedom—but if he chose to join issue, they would have the case tried in the Supreme Court; but this proposition the Captain declined: he knew well enough that it would result in my favor; and after some flattery and coaxing, he left me with my friend, Mr. Comstock, in liberty and peace!

CHAPTER FIVE

A Kidnapping

The business affairs of Capt. Helm had for some time been far from prosperous; and now he was quite poor. . . .

He had no partiality for labor of any kind; horse-racing and card-playing were far more congenial to his tastes; reduced as he now was, he would deny himself no luxury that his means or credit would procure. His few remaining slaves were given into the hands of an idle, brutal overseer—while they, half fed, half clothed, grew more and more discontented, and ran away on every opportunity that offered.

The Captain at last hit upon a method of making money, which, if it had been carried into operation on the high seas, would in all probability have been called by its right name, and incurred the penalty of the gallows—as piracy. . . .

The Captain's plan was to collect all the slaves he had once owned, many of whom had escaped to the surrounding villages, and when once in his grasp, to run them speedily into a slave state [a Southern state where Slavery was legal], and there sell them for the Southern market.

This building (left), located in Alexandria, Georgia, is an example of where slave dealers sold slaves. Inside the building (right), the slaves stood on platforms to be sold.

To carry forward this hellish design, it was necessary to have recourse to stratagem [a plan]. Some person must be found to lure the unsuspecting slaves into the net he was spreading for them. At last he found a scoundrel named Simon Watkins, who for the consideration of fifty dollars, was to collect as many of the slaves as he could at one place; and when he had done so, he was to receive the money, leaving Capt. Helm to do the rest.

Simon set immediately about the business, which was first to . . . in great kindness and generosity, give a large party to the colored people—desiring that all Capt. Helm's former slaves, in particular, should be present to have a joyous re-union, and celebrate their freedom in having a fine time generally.

Invitations were sent to all, and extensive preparation made for a large "social party" . . . at the house of Mrs. Bristol. My parents [who were also in the North] were invited; and Simon took the pains . . . to give me a special invitation. When the time arrived

for the party, I went to Palmyra with the intention of attending. I had not the least suspicion of any wrong; yet, by some mysterious providence, or something for which I can not account, a presentiment took possession of my mind that all was not right. I knew not what I feared, and could in no way define my apprehensions; but I grew so uneasy, that I finally gave up the party and returned home, before the guests were assembled.

Capt. Helm and his assistants came on to Palmyra in disguise, before evening, and secreted themselves in one of the hotels to await the arrival of their victims. At the appointed hour the slaves began to assemble in large numbers and great glee, without the least suspicion of danger. They soon began their amusements, and in the midst of their mirth, Capt. Helm and party stealthily crept from their hiding

Once freed, slaves sang in choruses, held their own religious prayer meetings, and worked in the fields like any other free person. They liked to celebrate their freedom.

31

place and surrounded the house; then bursting in suddenly upon the revelers, began to make arrests. Such a tumult, such an affray as ensued would be hard to describe.

The slaves fought for their lives and their liberty, and the Captain's party for their property and power. Fists, clubs, chairs, and anything they could get hold of, [were] freely used with a strength and will of men who had tested the joys of freedom. Cries and curses were mingled, while blows fell like hail on both sides. Commands from our old master were met with shouts of bold defiance on the part of the Negroes, until the miserable kidnappers were glad to desist, and were driven off—not stealthily as they came, but in quick time and in the best way they could, to escape the threatened vengeance of the slaves. . . .

Though he failed that night, Captain Helm didn't give up on his scheme. He and his men kidnapped a number of freed slaves in New York State and tried to take them South to sell them. Along the route, the former slaves rebelled and all but two children escaped. Captain Helm was later tried and convicted of kidnapping but no fine or penalty was ever imposed.

Later, several of Steward's abolitionist friends helped him start a grocery business, which eventually became quite successful. However, he was not content to enjoy his freedom while other slaves suffered. In the 1830s, he eventually went to Canada where he helped establish a haven for runaway slaves.

Source: Steward, Austin. *Twenty-two Years a Slave, and Forty Years a Freeman.* Rochester, NY: William Alling, 1857.

Louis Hughes

PART TWO

From Freedom to Slavery

CHAPTER ONE

It was difficult for a slave or even a free African-American to escape the snare of unscrupulous slave traders (individuals who captured and sold slaves) and slave owners. At times free African-Americans in the north were kidnapped or otherwise tricked into coming South only to be illegally kept in bondage.

In some cases, slaves who were to be set free upon their owner's death were illegally kept by relatives who purposefully "lost" these documents. In other instances, slaves brought north with their owners for extended periods should have been freed according to the laws of that state. However, too often many slave owners ignored these laws.

Louis Hughes and his wife, Matilda, were slaves. However, according to the laws of the Northern states, they should not have been. Hughes recounts Matilda's story first.

My wife Matilda was born in Fayette county, Kentucky, June 17th, 1830. It seems that her mother and her seven chil-

dren were to have been free according to the old Pennsylvania law.

There were two uncles of the family who were also to have been free, but who had been kept over time; so they sued for their freedom, and gained it. The lawyers in the case were abolitionists and friends to the slaves, and saw that these men had justice.

After they had secured their freedom, they entered suit for my

Louis Hughes

wife's mother, their sister, and her seven children. But as soon as the brother entered this suit, Robert Logan, who claimed my wife's mother and her children as his slaves, put them into a trader's yard in Lexington; and when he saw that there was a possibility of their being successful in securing their freedom, he put them in jail, to be "sold down the river" [sold to do hard labor on the plantations of the Deep South].

This was a deliberate attempt to keep them from their rights, for he knew they were to have been set free, many years before, and this fact was known to all the neighborhood. My wife's mother was born free, her mother, having passed the allotted time under a law, had been free for many years. Yet they kept her children as slaves, in plain violation of law as well as justice. The children of free persons under Southern laws were free—this was always admitted. The course of Logan in putting the family in jail, for safe keeping until they could be sent to the Southern market, was a tacit admission that he had no legal hold upon them.

Woods and Collins, a couple of . . . [slave] traders, were collecting a "drove" [a large group] of slaves for Memphis, about this time, and, when they were ready to start, all the family were sent off with the gang; and, when they arrived in Memphis, they were put in the traders' yard. . . .

None of this family were sold to the same person except my wife and one sister. All the rest were sold to different persons. The elder daughter was sold seven times in one day. The reason of this was that the parties that bought her, finding that she was

A slave auction from the nineteenth century

not legally a slave, and that they could get no written guarantee that she was, got rid of her as soon as possible. It seems that those who bought the other members of the family were not so particular, and were willing to run the risk. They knew that such things—such outrages upon law and justice—were common. Among these was my Boss [Mr. Jack McGee, or old Jack], who bought two of the girls, Matilda and her sister Mary Ellen. Matilda was bought for a cook. . . .

I remember well the day she came. The madam greeted her, and said: "Well, what can you do, girl? Have you ever done any cooking? Where are you from?" Matilda was, as I remember her, a sad picture to look at. She had been a slave, it is true, but had seen good days to what the slaves down the river saw. Any one could see she was almost heartbroken—she never seemed happy. Days grew into weeks and weeks into months, but the same routine of work went on.

Life as a New Slave

CHAPTER TWO

Matilda had been there three years when I married her. . . .
Things went on as usual after this. The madam grew more irri-
table and exacting, always finding fault with the servants,
whipping them, or threatening to do so, upon the slightest
provocation, or none at all. There was something in my wife's
manner, however, which kept the madam from whipping her—
an open or implied threat perhaps that such treatment would
not be endured without resistance or protest of some kind.

This the madam regarded as a great indignity, and she
hated my wife for it, and, at times, was ready to crush her, so
great was her anger. In a year there were born to us twin ba-
bies; and the madam now thought she had my wife tied, as the
babies would be a barrier to anything like resistance on her
part, and there would be no danger of her running away. She,
therefore, thought that she could enjoy, without hindrance, the
privilege of beating the woman of whose womanhood she had
therefore stood somewhat in fear.

Boss said from the first that I should give my wife assistance, as she needed time to care for the babies. Really he was not as bad as the madam at heart, for she tried to see how hard she could be on us. She gave me all the extra work to do that she could think of, apparently to keep me from helping my wife in the kitchen. She had all the cooking to do for three heavy meals

A slave mother and her two children

each day, all the washing and ironing of the finest clothes, besides caring for the babies between time.

In the morning she would nurse the babies, then hurry off to the kitchen to get breakfast while they were left in charge of a little girl. Again at noon she repeated her visit to the babies, after cooking the dinner, then in the evening, after supper, she would go to nurse them again. After supper was over, dishes all washed and kitchen in order, she would then go to the little ones for the night. One can see that she had very little time with the

A slave mother washes her master's clothes while her children help with some chores.

children. My heart was sore and heavy, for my wife was almost run to death with work.

The children grew puny and sickly for want of proper care. The doctor said it was because the milk the mother nursed to them was so heated by her constant and excessive labors as to be unwholesome, and she never had time to cool before ministering to them. So the little things, instead of thriving and developing, as was their right, dwindled toward the inevitable end. Oh! we were wretched—our hearts ached for a day which we could call our own. My wife was a Christian, and had learned to know the worth of prayer, so would always speak consolingly. "God will help us," she said: "let us try and be patient."

Our trial went on, until one morning I heard a great fuss in the house, the madam calling for the yard man to come and tie

my wife, as she could not manage her. My wife had always re-
fused to allow the madam to whip her; but now, as the babies
were here, mistress thought she would try it once more. Matilda
resisted, and madam called for Boss. In a minute he came,
and, grabbing my wife, commenced choking her, saying to her:
"What do you mean? Is that the way you talk to ladies?" My
wife had only said to her mistress: "You shall not whip me."
This made her furious, hence her call for Boss. I was in the din-
ing room, and could hear everything. My blood boiled in my
veins to see my wife so abused; yet I dare not open my mouth.

After the fuss, my wife went straight to the laundry. I fol-
lowed her there, and found her bundling up her babies' clothes,
which were washed but not ironed. I knew at a glance that she
was going away. Boss had just gone to the city; and I did not
know what to say, but I told her to do the best she could.

Often when company came and I held the horses, or did an
errand for them, they would tip me to a quarter or half a dollar.
This money I always saved, and so had a little change, which I
now gave to Matilda, for her use in her effort to get away from
her cruel treatment.

She started at once for . . . [the slave] trader's yards, with the
babies in her arms and, after she got into Memphis, she stopped
outside the yard to rest. While she was sitting on the curb stone,
Forrest [a slave trader] came out of the yard by the back gate
and saw her.

Coming up to her he said: "My God! Matilda, what are
you doing here? You have changed so I could not have known

you. Why have you come here?" Matilda said: "I came back here to be sold again."

Matilda went to the slave trader to offer herself to be sold in hopes of finding a better master. At that point she must have felt that any situation she and her children fell into would be better than the one they had.

He stepped back and called another . . . [slave] trader, Collins by name, from Kentucky. "Look here," said Forrest, pointing to my wife. Collins took in the situation at once and said he would buy her and the children. "That woman is of a good family," he said, "and was only sold to prevent her from getting her freedom." She was then taken into the yard. . . . Word was then sent McGee that his cook was in the yard and had come to be sold. He went in haste to the yard. Collins offered to buy her, but McGee said no man's money could buy that woman and her children. . . .

Hughes' wife was taken home and punished. It was clear that at least for now she would remain with their present owner.

The Civil War

CHAPTER THREE

The situation would change with the start of the Civil War in 1861. Abraham Lincoln, the presidential candidate who declared that the country could not go on indefinitely as a half-free, half-slave nation, had been elected president the year before. Intent on preserving their way of life with slavery, eleven Southern states eventually seceded from the Union, forming the Confederate States of America. To preserve the Union, Lincoln declared war on the Confederate States.

As slave owners feared, many slaves ran off to join the Union army. This served to deplete the Confederate army's resources and strengthen the enemy. Their worries intensified on January 1, 1863, when President Lincoln issued the Emancipation Proclamation, officially freeing all slaves everywhere, including those in Confederate territory.

Back at home, Louis Hughes and his wife were forcibly kept on the plantation, even after the Emancipation Proclamation had freed all the slaves. They feared that they would be murdered.

Abraham Lincoln (1809–1865), the sixteenth
president of the United States

*It was about this time, that the
law or regulation of the rebel [Con-
federate] government was promul-
gated [made known], authorizing or
directing the shooting or hanging of
any slave caught trying to get away
to the Union army. This barbarous
law was carried out in many cases,
for every little while we would hear of
some slave who was caught running
away, and hung or shot.*

*Two slaves belonging to one Wal-
lace, one of our nearest neighbors, had tried to escape to the
Union soldiers, but were caught, brought back and hung. All of
our servants were called up, told every detail of the runaway
and capture of the poor creatures and their shocking murder,
and then compelled to go and see them where they hung. I never
shall forget the horror of the scene—it was sickening.*

*We longed for freedom, but were content for the time with
hoping and praying for the coming of the day when it should be
realized. . . .*

*We had remained at old Jack's [the master, McGee] until
June 1865, and had tried to be content. The Union soldiers were
still raiding all through that section. Every day some town
would be taken, and the slaves would secretly rejoice. After we
came back from Alabama we were held with a tighter rein than
ever. We were not allowed to go outside of the premises.*

When the Civil War began, slaves joined the Union army to escape from slavery. Pictured left, an escaped slave stands in his Union uniform. For the slaves, this became an opportunity to fight against those who made them slaves. The 54th Massachusetts Black Regiment, pictured right, was one black regiment that many slaves had joined. They won several battles, including one in 1863 at Fort Wagner, near Charleston, South Carolina.

George Washington, a fellow servant, and Kitty, his wife, and I had talked considerably about the Yankees, and how we might get away. We knew it was our right to be free, for the proclamation had long been issued—yet they still held us. I did not talk much to my wife about going away, as she was always so afraid I would be killed, and did not want me to try any more to escape. But George, his wife and I continued to discuss the matter, whenever we had a chance. We knew that Memphis was headquarters for the Union troops, but how to reach it was the great question.

It was Sunday, and I had driven one portion of the family to church, and George the other . . . George came out, and finding me, told me what they had said. "No slave from outside is to be allowed on the place," said he. I replied: "If we listen to them we shall be here until Christmas comes again." "What do you mean?" asked George. "I mean that now, today, is the time to make a start."

So, late in the afternoon, during the servants' prayer meeting . . . we thought would be a good time to get away, as no one would be likely to see us. We talked with John Smith, another servant, and told him all about our plan, asking him not to say a word about our being gone until he was through feeding the stock. This would give us another hour to advance on our journey, as the feeding usually took about that time—from six o'clock until seven. Our fear was that we might be overtaken by the bloodhounds; and, therefore, we wished to get as far away as possible before the white people knew we were gone.

It was Sunday afternoon, June 26th, 1865, when George and I, having made ready for the start for the Union lines, went to bid our wives good-bye. I told my wife to cheer up, as I was coming again to get her. I said to Kitty, George's wife: "We are going, but look for us again. It will not be with us as with so many others, who have gone away, leaving their families and never returning for them. We will be here again." She looked up at me, smiling and with a look of resolution, said: "I'll be ready."

She was of a firm, daring nature—I did not fear to tell her all my plans. As my wife was so timid, I said as little as possible to her. George and I hurriedly said farewells to our wives. The parting was heart-rending, for we knew the dangers were great, and the chances were almost even that we should not meet again. I could hardly leave my wife, her agitation and grief were so great. But we were off in a few moments.

We crept through the orchard, passing through farm after farm until we struck the railroad, about seven miles from home. We followed this road until we reached Senatobia [Mississippi], about half past seven in the evening. We felt good, and, stopping all night, we started the next morning for Hernando, Miss., another small town, and reached there at two o'clock in the afternoon.

The most of the bridges had been burned, by the troops, and there were no regular railroad trains. Fortunately, however, flat cars drawn by horses were run over the road; and on a train of this kind we took passage. On several occasions, the passengers had to get out, and push the car over a bridge, as it was not made so horses could cross on it, the horses meantime being driven or led through the stream, and then hitched to the car again. After we had gone through this process repeatedly, we at last reached Memphis, arriving about seven o'clock Monday evening. The city was filled with slaves, from all over the South, who cheered and gave us a welcome.

Freedom at Last

I could scarcely recognize Memphis, things were so changed. [Many of the runaway slaves had gathered in Memphis seeking the protection of Union forces.] We met numbers of our fellow servants who had run away before us, when the war began. Tuesday and Wednesday we spent in making inquires . . . Thursday we went to see Col. Walker, a Union officer, who looked after the colored folks, and saw that they had their rights. When we reached his office we found it so filled with people, waiting to see him, that we were delayed about two hours, before we had an opportunity of speaking with him. When our turn came, we went in, and told him . . .

"Colonel, we want protection to go back to Mississippi after our wives, who are still held as slaves." He replied: "You are both free men to go and come as you please." "Why," said I, "Colonel, if we go back to Mississippi they will shoot the gizzards out of us." "Well," said he, "I can not grant your request. I would be overrun with similar applications." . . . We thanked him and left.

Slaves fled to the Union army for protection.

*After carefully considering the matter, we concluded to go
back to Senatobia and see the captain of the Union troops
there. The next day, Friday, we hired a two-horse wagon, and
made preparations to start on our perilous undertaking Saturday morning. It was our hope to find someone at Senatobia to
go with us . . . and protect us in the effort to bring away our
wives. . . .*

The men found two Union soldiers with some free time who
were willing to accompany them back to their former owner's plantation.

*After a long and weary ride we reached old Master Jack's a
little after sundown. The soldiers rode into the yard ahead of us,
and the first person they met was a servant (Frank) at the wood-*

pile. They said to him: "Go in and tell your master, Mr. McGee, to come out, we want to see him," at the same time asking for Louis' and George's wives. Young William McGee came out and the soldiers said to him, "We want feed for seventy-five head of horses." McGee said: "We have not got it." Just then George and I were coming up. We drove in at the gate, through the grove, and passed the woodpile where McGee and the soldiers were talking. McGee had just replied: "We have not got that much feed to spare—we are almost out." "Well," said the soldiers, "We must have it," and they followed on right after [our] wagon.

As soon as George and I drove up to the first cabin, which was my wife's and Kitty's, we ran in. Kitty met us at the door and said: "I am all ready." She was looking for us. We commenced loading our wagon with our few things.

Meanwhile the soldiers had ridden around a few rods and came upon old Master Jack and the minister of the parish, who were watching as guards to keep the slaves from running away to the Yankees. . . . As the soldiers rode up to the two men they said: "Hello! What are you doing here? Why have you not told these two men, Louis and George, that they are free men—that they can go and come as they like?"

By this time all the family were aroused, and great excitement prevailed. The soldiers' presence drew all the servants near. George and I hurried to fill up our wagon, telling our wives to get in, as there was no time to lose—we must go at once. In twenty minutes we were all loaded. My wife . . . Kitty and nine other servants followed the wagon.

With hardly any possessions, slaves fled to be free.

I waited for a few moments for Mary Ellen, sister of my wife; and as she came running out of the white folks' house, she said to her mistress . . . : "Good-bye; I wish you good luck." "I wish you all the bad luck," said she in a rage. But Mary did not stop to notice her mistress further; and, joining me, we were soon on the road following the wagon.

Those soldiers were brave indeed. Think of the courage and daring involved in this scheme—only two soldiers going into a country of which they knew nothing except that every white man living in it was their enemy. The demand which they made for food for seventy-five horses was a clever ruse [trick], invented by them to alarm the McGees, and make them think that there was a troop of horses near by, and that it would not be safe for them to offer any resistance to our going away with our wives. Had they thought that there were but two soldiers, it is certain that they would have endeavored to prevent us getting away again, and one or more of us would undoubtedly have been killed.

As already stated, nine other slaves followed our wagon, as it moved off. They had no hats on; some were bare-footed—they had not stopped to get anything; but, as soon as they saw a chance to get away, they went just as they were at the moment. . . .

After securing their freedom, Louis Hughes and his wife lived in the North where they were reunited with others in their families. Hughes attended night school and later owned and operated a large laundry business.

Source: Hughes, Louis. *Thirty Years a Slave, From Bondage to Freedom*. Milwaukee, WI: South Side Printing Co., 1897.

Bethany Veney

PART THREE

Family Life

The family life of a slave was never secure. Slave families could be torn apart at any moment and for any reason: the whim of the owner, the owner's death, the owner's financial problems, or even if a member of slave's family ran away.

Slaves were allowed and sometimes even encouraged to marry because the slave couple's children would only enhance the owner's personal wealth. Yet the owners did not recognize these marriages when it did not suit them. Bethany Veney describes the devastating effects this had on her family and life.

> *I have but little recollection of my very early life. My mother and her five children were owned by one James Fletcher, Pass Run, town of Luray, Page County, Virginia. Of my father I know nothing. . . .*
>
> *The next thing I recall as being of any particular importance to me was the death of my mother, and, soon after, that of Master Fletcher. I must have been about nine years old at that time.*

Master's children consisted of five daughters and two sons. As usual in such cases, an inventory was taken of his property (all of which nearly was in slaves), and being apportioned in shares, lots were drawn, and, as might chance, we fell to our several masters and mistresses.

Bethany Veney

My sister Matilda and myself were drawn by the eldest daughter, Miss Lucy . . . but . . . after a time she married David Kibbler, and . . . went to live with [him], taking her human property with her, to wait on her, and also to work for Mr. Kibbler. . . .

Poor Miss Lucy! She was kind and tender-hearted. She often said she hated slavery, and wanted nothing to do with it; but she could see no way out of it. . . . Miss Lucy now told me, if I would be contented and stay quietly where I was, and not be married, she would, when her nephew Noe came to be of age, give me my freedom. Instead of this, however, I was told soon after that she had made her will, bequeathing me already to this nephew. I was never sure this was true. Her kindness to me and my love for her made it always seem impossible.

But as she relates in her narrative, despite Miss Lucy's instructions, Bethany did eventually marry.

In a slave wedding, the couple stepped over a broomstick. It represented stepping into their new life as husband and wife.

Year after year rolled on. Master Jonas Mannyfield lived seven miles from us . . . and he owned a likely young fellow called Jerry. We had always known each other, and now he wanted to marry me. Our masters were both willing. . . . So it happened, one day, there was a colored man—a peddler, with his cart—on the road, and Jerry brought him in, and said he was ready to be minister for us. He asked us a few questions, which we answered in a satisfactory manner, and then he declared us husband and wife. I did not want him to make us promise that we would always be true to each other, forsaking all others, as the white people do in their marriage service, because I knew that at any time our masters could compel us to break such a promise . . . Jerry and I were happy as, under all the circumstances, we could be. . . .

If two married slaves were owned by different owners, the slaves lived separately at each owner's plantation. Whenever they wanted to visit or spend time with each other, they had to ask their owners' permission.

Eight or ten months passed on, when one night my brother Stephen, who lived on the Blue Ridge, near Master Mannyfield, came to see me, and, as we talked of many things, he spoke of Jerry in a way that instantly roused my suspicion. I said: "Tell me what is the matter? I know there is some thing. Is Jerry dead? Is he sold? Tell me what it is." I saw he dreaded to speak, and that frightened me the more.

At last, he said: "This [is] no use, Betty. You have got to know it. Old Look-a-here's people are all in jail for debt." "Old Look-a-here" was the nickname by which Mannyfield was known by the colored people far and near, because he had a way of saying, when he was about to whip one of his slaves, "Now look-a-here, you black rascal," or "you black wench."

A newspaper advertisement about the sale of a deceased owner's property, including slaves and animals

Since slaves were considered property, slaves could be seized and sold to pay their owner's debts.

The next day was Saturday, and I hurried to complete my task in the corn-field, and then asked my master if I could go to see Jerry. He objected at first, but at last gave me a pass to see my brother, and be gone until Monday morning. [Slaves travel- ing alone were required to carry passes from their masters to prove they were not runaways.] The sun might have been two hours high when I started; but before I was half over the moun- tain, night had closed round me its deepest gloom. The vivid flashes of lightning made the carriage path plain at times, and then I could not see a step before me; and the rolling thunder added to my fear and dread. I was dripping wet when about nine o'clock, I reached the house.

It had been my plan to get Stephen to go on with me to Jerry's mother's and stay the night there; but his mistress, who was sister to my Miss Lucy, declared we must not go on in the storm and, giving me supper, brought bedding, that I might lie on the kitchen floor and rest me there. In the morning, after a good breakfast, she started us off, with a bag of biscuits to eat by the way. Jerry's mother was glad to go with us; and we hur- ried along to Jerry, in jail at Little Washington were he with his fellow-slaves was confined, like sheep or oxen, shut up in stalls, to be sold to pay their owner's debts.

Jerry saw us, as we came along the road, through the prison bars; and the jailor allowed us to talk together there, not, however, without a witness to all we might say. We had committed no offense against God or man. Jerry had not; and yet, like base criminals, we were denied even the consolation of privacy. . . .

Fleeing to Safety

Several months passed, and Mannyfield was still unable to redeem his property; and they [the slaves] were at last put up at auction and sold to the highest bidder. Frank White, a slave-trader, bought the entire lot, and proceeded at once to make up a gang for the Southern market.

Slave traders sometimes bought up sizable groups of slaves to meet the needs of large plantation owners in the Deep South.

Arrangements were made to start Friday morning; and on Thursday afternoon, chained together, the gang [was] taken across the stream, and encamped on its banks. White then went to Jerry, and taking the handcuffs from his wrists, told him to go and stay the night with his wife, and see if he could persuade her to go with him. If he could he would buy her [from her owner], and so they need not be separated. He would pass that way in the morning, and see. Of course, Jerry was only too glad to come; and, at first, I thought I would go with him . . .

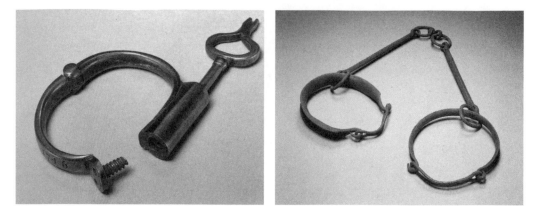

Various irons were used to keep slaves from running away while traveling.

After thinking it over though, Bethany realized that she would be better off declining Frank White's offer. As a slave, she had no assurances that she and her husband would be sold together and felt it was far more likely that she would simply go to the highest bidder. Instead, she and Jerry tried to think of another way they could stay together.

Then came the wish to secrete [hide] ourselves together in the mountains, or elsewhere, till White should be gone; but, to do this, detection was sure. Then we remembered that White had trusted us, in letting him come to me, and we felt ashamed, for a moment, as if we had tried to cheat; but what right had White to carry him away, or even to own him at all? We at last decided that, as soon as it was light, Jerry should take to the mountains, and, when White was surely gone, either I would join him there, and we would make for the North together, or he would come back, go to White's mother, who lived a few miles distant, and tell her he would work for her and obey her, but he would never go South [the deep South—Alabama, Mississippi, Louisiana, etc.] to be worked to death in the rice-swamps or cotton fields.

We talked late into the night, and at last, in the silence and dread, worn out with sorrow and fear, my head on his shoulder, we both dropped asleep. Daylight was upon us when we waked . . . "Have no fear," I said. "Go right along." . . . And, with a bound, he was over the fence, into the fields, and off to the mountains.

In a very short time, White and his poor, doomed company came along, and called Jerry. I had taken my pail to milk the cows; and, seeing me, he sung out, "Woman, where is Jerry, I say?" "I don't know where Jerry is," I answered. White then turned to me, and said, "I took off his handcuffs, and let him go to you, and you had no business to serve me so."

It was true, I did not know where Jerry was at that time. We had agreed that we would meet that night near the blacksmith's old shop . . . and that was all I knew of his

The South depended heavily upon the production of rice and cotton. Here slaves are picking cotton in the fields. In this photo an overseer on horseback watches the slaves as they work hard.

whereabouts, though he had not been gone long enough to be far away. It was true he had trusted us, and I felt very badly; but what else could we have done?

I then told him that Jerry had said he was willing to work, and would go to his mother's and serve her, but never, if he could help it, would he be carried South. Then White tried to bargain with Kibbler for my purchase, saying he would give any price he should name for me, because he knew I would then find Jerry. But it was no use. Kibbler had a kind spot in his heart, and would not consent to let me go. So the slave-trader moved on with his human cattle.

Five miles on the road lived David McCoy, another slave-trader. When White reached his house, it was agreed by them that, if McCoy could find Jerry within two days, he should bring him on, and they would meet at Stanton, Va.

The place where I was to meet Jerry was, as I have said, across the run, in a corn-field, near the blacksmith's shop, the time Friday night. It had rained hard all day, and the stream was swollen, and pouring and rushing at a fearful rate. I waited till everybody was in bed and asleep . . . and started for the Pass. It was still raining, and the night was very dark. Only by my torch could I see a step before me; and, when I attempted to wade in, as I did in many different places, I found it was no use. I should surely be drowned if I persisted. So, disappointed and grieved, I gave up and went home. The next morning I was able to get over on horseback to milk the cows, but I neither heard nor saw anything of Jerry.

Facing the Truth

CHAPTER THREE

Saturday night came. I knew well that, if not caught by White, Jerry would be round. At least, every one was in bed, and all was still. I waited and listened. I listened and waited. Then I heard his step at the door. I hurriedly opened it, and he came in. His clothes were still damp and stiff from the rain of yesterday. He was frightened and uneasy. He had been hiding around in different places, constantly fearing detection. He had seen me from behind the old blacksmith's shop when I had tried the night before . . . to ford the stream; and he was glad, he said, when he saw me go back, for he knew I should be carried down by the current and be drowned, if I had persisted.

I went to my mistress' bedroom, and asked her if I might go to the cellar. She knew at once what I meant, and whispered softly, "Betty, has Jerry come?" Then, without waiting for reply, added, "get him some milk and light bread and butter." I was not long in doing so; and the poor fellow ate like one famishing. Then he wanted to know all that had happened, and what

White had said when he found he was gone. We talked a long time, and tried to devise some plans for our mutual safety and possible escape from slavery altogether; but, every way we looked, the path was beset with danger and exposure. We were both utterly disheartened. But sleep came at last and, for the time being, relieved us of our fears.

In the morning, which was Sunday, we had our breakfast together, and, as the hours passed, began to feel a little comforted. After dinner, we walked out to the field and strolled about for some time; and, when ready to go back to the house, we each took an armful of fodder [food] along for the horses. As we laid it down and turned to go into the house, David McCoy rode up on horseback. He saw Jerry at once, and called him to come to the fence. The excitement of the last days—the fasting and the fear—had completely cowed and broken whatever of manhood, or even of brute courage, a slave might by any possibility be presumed at any time to be possessed of, and the last remains of these qualities in poor Jerry were gone. He mutely obeyed; and when, with an oath, McCoy commanded him to mount the horse behind him, he mutely seated himself there.

McCoy then called to me to go to the house and bring Jerry's clothes. "Never," I screamed back to him, "never, not to save your miserable life." But Jerry said: "O Betty, 'tis no use. We can't help it."

I knew this was so. I stifled my anger and my grief, brought his little bundle, into which I tucked a testament and catechism someone had given me, and shook hands "good-by" with him. So we parted forever, in this world.

64

Slaves tried to escape into the swamps, the mountains, or the rivers—anywhere they could.

Veney was pregnant when Jerry was taken away. Soon afterwards she gave birth to a little girl. When she and her daughter were later sold as a pair, she was relieved that they had not been separated. Yet her good fortune did not last. In the years that followed, she was sold again and taken away from her daughter, but this time she knew the buyer all too well—the slave trader David McCoy.

Veney later met her second husband, Frank Veney, with whom she had a son. But after a time, her owner, McCoy, suffered some financial loses. Just as she was about to be sold once again, she was rescued by some Northerners in 1858 whom she had hired herself out to during their stay in the South. At times slaves were permitted to act as free agents. They could hire themselves out to others— giving the bulk of their wages to their owners. The Northerners purchased Veney and her son and brought them North to freedom.

Home in the North

The feelings with which I entered my Northern home, 22 Charlesfield Street, Providence, R.I., on a bright pleasant morning in August 1858, can be more easily fancied than described. A new life had come to me. I was in a land where, by its laws, I had the same right to myself that any other woman had. No jailer could take me to prison, and sell me at auction to the highest bidder. My boy was my own, and no one could take him from me.

But I had left behind me every one I had ever known. I did not forget the dreadful hardships I had endured, and yet somewhat I did not think of them with half the bitterness with which I had endured them. I was a stranger in a strange land; and it was no wonder, perhaps, that a dreadful loneliness and homesickness came over me . . . I couldn't help feeling bewildered sometimes at the difference in so many ways, and for a moment wished myself back in "old Virginia," with my own people; and I very, very often longed to see the old familiar faces and hear the old sounds, but

Here slaves reaching freedom are greeted by former slaves on their arrival in the north.

never could I forget to be grateful for my escape from a system under which I had suffered so much.

Following the Civil War and slavery's end, Veney ventured south to find her family and friends.

I had saved some money; and, as soon as it was deemed safe by my friends, I undertook the journey. . . . I found my daughter Charlotte grown to womanhood, married, and had one child. . . . After visiting about for six or seven weeks, I turned my face again to the North—my daughter, her husband and child coming with me. Three times since I have made the same journey, bringing back with me, from time to time, in all sixteen of my relatives, and

After the Civil War, freedom allowed slaves to do what they wanted. A husband and wife got their picture taken. A young family owned their own home.

have encountered many interesting incidents. I have always found some one—sometimes a policeman, and sometimes a simple woman or boy—ready and willing to help me in every emergency, when I had need. I have great reason to speak well of my fellow-men, and to be most thankful to the overruling Providence that brought me up out of the "house of bondage."

By the time she was seventy-four years old, Veney owned her own home in the North as well as another nearby house where her daughter and grandchildren resided. Veney lived the rest of her life surrounded by family—a sharp contrast to what her years in bondage had been like.

Source: Veney, Bethany. *The Narrative of Bethany Veney, A Slave Woman*, 2nd ed. Worcester, MA, 1890.

James L. Smith

PART FOUR

Limited Freedom

Born in Virginia in 1881, James L. Smith was not very useful as a field hand due to an early leg injury. So his owner had him trained as a shoemaker and allowed him to hire himself out to others. Nearly all his earnings went to his owner, but there were tremendous advantages to Smith's situation. He was allowed to live off the plantation and, therefore, was not strictly supervised by an overseer. After proving himself both efficient and trustworthy, Smith was allowed to come and go as he pleased. This freedom, denied to most slaves in more typical situations, was instrumental in his escape to freedom.

> *I became acquainted with a man by the name of Zip, who was a sailor; I told him my object in reference to freedom. [Like Smith, Zip functioned as a free agent hiring himself out to others.] He told me that he also was intending to make his escape to have his freedom. This was in the year 1836. We agreed that whenever there was a chance we would come off together.*

About Christmas, 1837, we made an arrangement to run away. Zip was calculating to take the vessel that the white people had left during their absence. He was left to take care of this vessel till they returned; nevertheless he intended to use it to a good purpose, for he took this opportunity to make his escape . . . but we were disappointed because

James L. Smith

we could not carry out our arrangements. It was a very cold Christmas Eve, so much so that the river was badly frozen, not making it favorable for us to capture her; hence we gave that project up until the spring of 1838.

On the 6th day of May, 1838, Zip, with another one by the name of Lorenzo and myself, each hired a horse to take a short journey up the country to Lancaster, to see a sick friend of ours, who was very ill. . . . In the afternoon we started for home, reaching there about four o'clock. . . .

Working as free agents all three could travel safely within the region. However, their status could change at any moment. Without their consent, they could be brought back to work as a plantation field hand or be sold.

When we reached Heathsville, the place where we lived, we noticed as we rode up to the stable to put the horses away, (for we were on horse-back) that there were half a dozen or more [white] young men, who appeared to be talking and whittling behind the stable. The stable where I put my horse was on one side of the street, and the stable where Zip was to put his was on the opposite side. Zip went up to the door to put his horse in, but found that it would not open readily, and while he was trying to open it those white young men whom we saw whittling, supposing that he had got in, began to assemble around the door.

Now among these young men was a Negro-trader who spoke to Zip, asking him "why he did not go in and put his horse away." Zip told him that "he could not get the door open." The trader then took hold of the door and it came open immediately. Zip was so astonished to think that the door opened so readily to the Negro-trader, and did not yield to him, that he thought there must be something wrong about it. He refused to go in himself, and only fastened the horse's bridle to a fence, then went over to the tavern to tell the hostler [one who takes care of horses] that he might put the horse away.

From there he went to his house and his wife warned him to flee for his life, for a trader had bought him [from his previous owner], and had been to the house with several young men whom we saw behind the stable as we rode up, [and who had] placed themselves there for the purpose of waiting till we came. Their motive was, when Zip went into the stable to close the door on him and capture him.

The cabin home where Smith lived

I knew nothing about this at the time. I put my horse away, went to the house, got something to eat, then started to go off some five miles to see some friends; but before I started I thought I would go into my shop and brush my coat; while there I sat down on my bench just for a few moments, and all at once I fell asleep. When I awoke the sun was just going down. I think I had been asleep about an hour. I did not have any idea of falling asleep when I entered the shop, for I intended to have gone out of town. As quick as thought I jumped up, took my hat and started for the door; just as I opened it there was a man passing by whose name was Griffin Muse, who belonged on James Smith's [no relation] plantation about two miles off.

He saw me as I opened the door, and said to me . . . "Where have you been? I have been looking for you this two hours. I just started to go down home and give up the search and to tell Zip that I could not find you." Said I, "What is the matter?" Said he to me, "did you not know that Zip was sold to a Georgian trader, who is trying to catch him." Said I, "where is Zip?" I am sure I did not know anything about this, I did not dream of such a thing; I saw this trader, with some young men behind the stable, but did not dream that he was after Zip. Griffin Muse said to me, "Zip is down on our plantation, and has sent me after you, and that his intention is to try to make his escape tonight to a free country, and if you are going with him to go to him as soon as possible."

I was so astonished that I did not know what to do. I told him to "wait for me, and I would get ready as soon as possible." I went a few blocks where I kept my box, and in it I had three dollars, all the money I possessed in the world. On my way back I met a man who owed me fifty cents; I dunned him, and as good luck would have it he had the money and paid me.

I then went back to my shop and picked up all the things that I thought I would want to take with me. While I was making my arrangements my boss came into the shop. As soon as I saw him coming I pushed my bundle under the bench and sat down on the bench, pretending to be sick. He asked me if I "was going to church"; I told him I thought "I should not, for I was not feeling very well." After a while he went out and closed the door after him. Soon as he was gone I finished gathering up my things, then locked up the shop and went into the "great house" to put the key over the mantle-piece. Then Griffin Muse, Zip's wife and myself started for Smith's plantation, about two miles from Heathsville, where Zip was secreted [hidden].

CHAPTER TWO

Sailing Away

When we arrived there Zip and Lorenzo were just starting; it was nearly eleven o'clock; they had waited for me till they thought I was not coming. They were just bidding the folks farewell as I arrived at the house where Zip stopped. Two minutes more and I would have been left behind. If I had not fallen asleep in the shop I would have been out of town, and I should have been left, for Griffin would not have found me; and if I had slept one minute longer he would have passed by the shop and I would not have seen him; one minute more, either way, would have turned the scales.

All three of us, Zip, Lorenzo and myself, assembled together and started for the Cone River, about a quarter of a mile from where we were. There were a number of our plantation friends who went with us; Zip's wife and her mother, and a number of others. When we came to the river, we stood on the beach and embraced, kissed, and bade each other farewell. The scene between Zip and his wife resounded in the depths of his heart; we could not take her with us for the boat was too small.

. . . We took a small canoe and crossed the river till we came to a plantation owned by a man named Travis. He had a large sail boat that we desired to capture, but we did not know how we should accomplish it, as they took a great deal of pains generally to haul her up, lock her up and put the sails and oars in the barn. As it was the Sabbath day, the young folks had been sailing about the river, and instead of securing her as they usually did, they left her anchored in the stream with the sails and oars all in the boat. This was very fortunate for us, for the house was very near to the shore, besides they had very savage dogs there. So it would have been a very difficult matter for us to attempt to capture the boat sails and oars if they had been where they were generally kept. So all we had to do was to run our canoe along side the boat and get on board.

It was quite calm before we started, but as soon as we got ready, and the sails set, the wind began to rise, and all that night we had all the wind we could carry sail to. Lorenzo and myself, by keeping our oars in motion, outran everything that stayed on the water. By the next morning we were a great distance from home. We sailed all day and night Monday, and until Tuesday night about nine o'clock, when we landed just below Frenchtown, Maryland. We there hauled the boat up the best we could, and fastened her, then took out bundles and started on foot. Zip, who has been a sailor from a boy, knew the country and understood where to go. He was afraid to go through Frenchtown, so we took a circuitous route, until we came to the road that leads from Frenchtown to New Castle.

Here I became so exhausted that I was obliged to rest; we went into the woods, which were near by, and laid down on the ground and slept for an hour or so, then we started for New Castle.

I found I could not keep up with my companions, for they could walk much faster than myself, and hence got far ahead, and then would have to wait for me; I being lame was not able to keep up with them. At last Zip said to me, " . . . we shall have to leave you for our enemies are after us, and if we wait for you we shall all be taken; so it would be better for one to be taken than all three." So after he had advised me what course to take, they started, and in a few minutes left me out of sight.

Smith, like the slave pictured above, tried not to be captured. He wanted to be free.

When I had lost sight of them I sat down by the road-side and wept, prayed, and wished myself back where I first started. I thought it was all over with me forever; I thought once I would

turn back as far as Frenchtown, and give myself up to be captured; then I thought that would not do; a voice spoke to me,
"not to make a fool of myself, you have got so far from home
(about two hundred and fifty miles), keep on towards freedom,
and if you are taken, let it be heading towards freedom." I then
took fresh courage and pressed my way onward towards the
north with anxious heart.

Finding Food

I was very hungry, for I had not eaten anything much for two days. We came away in such a hurry that we did not have time to prepare much food; we took only some corn-cake and a little bacon; I was almost starved to death; I became quite weak, and looked around on the ground to see if I could find anything green that I could eat. I began to fail very fast, I thought I should die there on the road.

All at once I came to a house, and a voice seemed to say to me, "go to that house and see if you can get something to eat." I said to myself, "there are white people that live there and I shall be captured. They can but capture me, and if I stay away I shall die." I went up to the door and rapped; a lady came to the door and looked at me with a smile upon her countenance as I spoke to her. I said to myself, "I do not mind you white people's smiles, I expect you think to make money off me this morning." I asked her if "she would give me something to eat." She said, "she had nothing cooked, but if I would come in she would get me something." I thought to myself, "I know what that means, you want me to come in in order to capture me"; but nevertheless I went in, and she set a chair up to the fireplace and bade me sit down.

Her husband sat there in one corner, and looking up said to me: "My man, you are traveling early this morning," I said "yes, I made an early start." (I did not tell him I had been traveling all day and all night for three nights.) He asked me "how far I was going," I told him, "I was going to Philadelphia; that I had some friends there whom I had not seen for some time, and I was going to visit them, and then return in a few weeks." Very soon his wife had my breakfast all ready of ham, eggs, and a meal-cake, and put them on the table, and then asked me to sit down. I did so, without waiting for a second invitation, and the first mouthful I took seemed to me as if it would go straight through me; I ate till I became alarmed, for I thought I would betray myself by my eating. I ate up most everything she put on the table, then I got up and asked "what I should pay for my breakfast," she said "twenty-five cents." I put my hand in my pocket and picked out a quarter, giving it to her, I started on my journey, feeling like a new man.

Reaching His Goal

I walked on till about noon, at which time I reached New Castle. The first one I saw was Lorenzo, who was one of the men who left me on the road. He came a little way out of the city to look for me, to see if I was any where in sight; we met and went into the city, found Zip, and once more we were together. The boat left there for Philadelphia twice a day. She had left in the morning before they had arrived, but she returned in the afternoon, only to start right off again the same afternoon.

By the time the boat had returned, I was there, so we three all went on board. How we ever passed through New Castle as we did, without being detected, is more than I can tell, for it was one of the worst slave towns in the country, and the law was such that no steamboat, or anything else, could take a colored person to Philadelphia without first proving his or her freedom.

Former slaves taking a boat to the North

Various localities passed legislation to restrict the movements of African-Americans in order to prevent escapes and uprising.

What makes it so astonishing to me is, that we walked aboard right in sight of every body, and no one spoke a word to us. We went to the captain's office and bought our tickets, without a word being said to us.

We arrived safely in Philadelphia that afternoon; there upon the wharf we separated, after bidding each other farewell. Lorenzo and Zip went on board a ship for Europe, and went to sea. I started up the street, not knowing where I was going, or what would become of me; I walked on till I came to a shoe

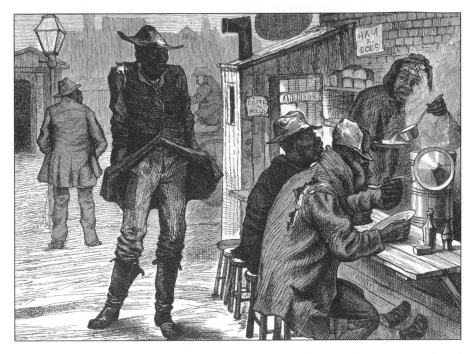

A former slave looks for something to eat in Philadelphia. (Drawing by S. G. McCutcheon)

store, went in and asked a white gentleman, "do you want to hire a shoe-maker?" He said "I do not, but think you can find a place by going a little further."

Although the next shoemaker did not hire Smith, he led him to a group of abolitionists who were quite helpful. They sent him to the home of Doctor Osgood, an abolitionist in Springfield, Massachusetts.

When I had reached the wharf I stepped ashore, and saw a man standing on the dock; and, after inquiries concerning Doctor Osgood's residence, he kindly showed it to me. The Doctor,

being at home, I gave him the letter [written by another aboli-
tionist explaining Smith's situation], and as soon as he had
read it, he and his family congratulated me on my escape from
the hand of the oppressor. He informed me that the letter stated
"that he could either send me to Canada, or he could keep me
in Springfield, just as he thought best." He said: "I think we will
keep you here, so you can make yourself at home." The family
gathered around me to listen to my thrilling narrative of escape.
We talked till the bell notified them that supper was ready. An
excellent meal was prepared for me, which I accepted gladly, for
the Doctor was a very liberal man, saying: "Friend, come in
and have some supper. . . ."

Doctor Osgood felt an interest in my safety, for my master
was on my track, and had advertised me through the press, try-
ing every means to get me, if possible. The Doctor secreted me in
a little room, called the fugitive's room. As I was secreted, all
schemes to capture were baffled.

After keeping me for a while, the Doctor endeavored to find
employment for me as a shoe-maker. He went to several per-
sons, but found none that would take me. Finally, for safety—
and the last resort—he went to see Mr. Elmore, an abolitionist,
who was a wholesale shoe dealer on Main Street. He readily
took me, saying: "Bring him to me, I want to see him." I went
to him one night with the Doctor, and he made a bargain with
me, and also gave me some work to do in his work-shop, se-
creted from public gaze. It was the first work I had ever done in
the like of a freed man, which gave me strength to think I was
a man with others. . . .

James L. Smith did well in the North. He established his own shoemaking business, married, and purchased his own home. Two of his daughters became teachers, while his son, James H. Smith, took up "the trade of his father."

Source: Smith, James L. *Autobiography of James L. Smith*. Norwich, CT: The Bulletin, 1881.

EPILOGUE

Slave narratives have an important place in our nation's history for a number of reasons. Prior to the Civil War, they played a vital role in the ongoing debate over slavery's existence in the United States. These autobiographies were the public's first opportunity to see slavery through the slave's eyes—adding an informative dimension to an issue often heatedly debated by businessmen, politicians, and everyday people. Certainly after reading these stories, it would be difficult to argue that African-Americans were happy in bondage or that they needed their master's guidance.

The majority of the slave narratives were published between 1830 and 1860, at the height of the abolitionist movement. This was a widespread antislavery movement that used any means at its disposal to advance its cause. In addition to helping slaves escape to the North, abolitionists assisted runaways in finding work and establishing new lives as free men and women. Often they asked former slaves to speak at their meetings, and in many instances, abolitionist presses published their narratives.

Two famous abolitionists were Frederick Douglass (1817–1895), pictured right, and John Brown (1800–1859), pictured left. Frederick Douglass published his own slave narrative in 1845, advised President Lincoln during the Civil War, and became the first black U.S. government official. John Brown wanted to win freedom for slaves. He caused an insurrection in Virginia in 1859, but was captured, tried, and hanged.

Through the years, some historians have argued that abolitionists actually wrote many of the existing former slave narratives. It's impossible to know whether the texts are in the words of the slaves themselves or in the words of the abolitionists who wrote everything down for some of the former slaves. In addition, did the abolitionists include their own thoughts in the narratives along with the slaves'? Yet even if a portion of abolitionist sentiment seeped through in some instances, the stories still ring painfully true. Many former slaves from varying parts of the South have described similar situations. Information regarding food, housing, work practices, and punishments have also been recovered from archeological evidence as well as from the records and diaries of slave-holding families.

While the slave narratives are factual, through the years they have inspired numerous works of fiction. Many plays and novels have been based on these accounts, creating art out of a largely political issue. This made the drama of slavery accessible to even greater numbers of people and it solidified the African-American's past as an undeniable part of America's history.

Collecting former slave narratives did not end with the abolitionist movement. Relatives of the slaves through the years continued to write down the histories. Also, during the 1930s, a number of students interviewed elderly African-Americans who had once been slaves. The largest number of these narratives recorded in modern times was collected during the Great Depression (1929–1939) through the Federal Writers Project, sponsored by the Work Projects Administration (WPA). Under its auspices, unemployed writers were sent out to interview former slaves using a specific set of questions.

Today, the former slave narratives are more important than ever. While these individuals are no longer here to tell their stories, their voices are heard. They present a revealing picture of a people in bondage, a brutal period in the history of our country, and inspiring stories that we cannot afford to forget.

FURTHER READINGS

Burchard, Peter. *Lincoln and Slavery*. New York: Atheneum, 1999.

Carbone, Elisa. *Stealing Freedom*. New York: Alfred A. Knopf, 1998.

Cox, Clinton. *Come All You Brave Soldiers: Blacks in the Revolutionary War*. New York: Scholastic Press, 1999.

Ferris, Jeri Chase. *With Open Hands: A Story About Biddy Mason*. Minneapolis, MN: Carolrhoda, 1999.

Hansen, Joyce. *Between Two Fires: Black Soldiers in the Civil War*. New York: Franklin Watts, 1993.

Hansen, Joyce, and Gary McGowen. *Breaking Ground, Breaking Silence: The Story of New York's African American Burial Ground*. New York: Henry Holt, 1998.

Haskins, James. *Bound for America: The Forced Migration of Africans to the New World*. New York: Lothrop, Lee & Shepard, 1999.

Hughes, Louis. *Thirty Years a Slave, From Bondage to Freedom*. Milwaukee, WI: South Side Printing Co., 1897.

Shnidman, Ellen. *The African American Answer Book*. New York: Chelsea House, 1998.

Smith, James L. *Autobiography of James L. Smith*. Norwich, CT: The Bulletin, 1881.

Steward, Austin. *Twenty-two Years a Slave, and Forty Years a Freeman*. Rochester, NY: William Alling, 1857.

Todras, Ellen H. *Angelina Grimke: Voice of Abolition*. North Haven, CN: Linnet, 1999.

Veney, Bethany. *The Narrative of Bethany Veney, A Slave Woman*. 2nd Ed. Worcester, MA, 1890.

Wilds, Mary. *The Life and Times of Elizabeth Freeman: The True Story of a Slave Who Won Her Freedom*. Greensboro, NC: Avisson, 1999.

Museums and Libraries

- Alexandria Black History Resource
  638 Alfred Street
  Alexandria, Virginia 22314

  A center containing books, photographs, paintings, and various pieces of memorabilia illustrating the role of African-Americans in Alexandria through the years.

- Amistad Research Center
  6823 St. Charles Avenue
  New Orleans, Louisiana 70118

  A substantial repository of primary source material on African-American history.

- Black Archives of Mid-America
  Fire Station 11
  Kansas City, Missouri 64108

  A center for artifacts and documents pertaining to African American history. It also sponsors workshops and exhibits.

- Northern California Center for African-American History and Life
  5606 San Pablo Avenue
  Oakland, California 94612

  A center with manuscripts, photographs, and oral histories documenting African-American life.

- Schomburg Center for Research in Black Culture
  The New York Public Library
  New York, New York 10037

  An outstanding research center for African-American studies. Its holdings include books, manuscripts, pamphlets, etchings, and photographs detailing the African-American's story in the United States.

Websites

- Getting Word: The Monticello African-American Oral History Project.
  www.monticello.org/gettingword

  Oral interviews with the descendants of Monticello slaves, spanning seven generations.

- Africans in America; America's Journey Through Slavery
  www.pbs.org/wgbh/aia

  A major collection of images, documents, stories, biographies, and commentaries.

- North American Slave Narratives, documenting the American South, at the University of North Carolina at Chapel Hill

  www.ibiblio.org/docsouth/fpn/texts.html

INDEX

ABOUT THE AUTHOR

Award-winning author Elaine Landau has a bachelors of art degree in English and journalism from New York University and a master's degree in library and information science from Pratt Institute. She worked as a newspaper reporter, a children's book editor, and a youth services librarian before becoming a full-time writer. Ms. Landau has written more than one hundred and fifty nonfiction books for young readers. She lives in Miami, Florida, with her husband, Norman, and son, Michael.